F-8 *Crusader* in Action

by Jim Sullivan

Color by Don Greer
Illustrated by Kevin Wornkey

squadron/signal publications
Aircraft Number 70

P9-DII-068

F-8J (149186) 'ROADRUNNER' of VF-211 flying from USS Hancock streaks by a North Viet-
namese MiG-17. VF-211 downed six MiGs during the air war over Vietnam. October 1968

F-8's FOREVER

WHEN YOU'RE OUT OF F-8's YOU'RE OUT OF FIGHTERS

COPYRIGHT © 1985 SQUADRON/SIGNAL PUBLICATIONS, INC.

1115 CROWLEY DRIVE, CARROLLTON, TEXAS 75011-5010
All rights reserved. No part of this publication may be reproduced, stored in a retrieval
system or transmitted in any form by any means electrical, mechanical or otherwise,
without written permission of the publisher.

ISBN 0-89747-168-7

If you have any photographs of the aircraft, armor, soldiers or ships of any nation, par-
ticularly wartime snapshots, why not share them with us and help make
Squadron/Signal's books all the more interesting and complete in the future. Any
photograph sent to us will be copied and the original returned. The donor will be fully
credited for any photos used. Please indicate if you wish us not to return the photos.
Please send them to: Squadron/Signal Publications, Inc., 1115 Crowley Dr., Carrollton, TX
75011-5010.

Dedication

This book is dedicated to the fighter pilots and ground crew who flew and
maintained the Chance Vought F8U Crusader, the Navy's first supersonic
jet fighter. Also to my Son, Jim Jr who is presently serving his Country in
the US Army.

Photo Credits

The author sincerely wished to thank all the people who provided photos
and other vital material toward the completion of this book. Special ap-
preciation is noted to Paul Bower and Al Ueckert of LTV Aerospace and
Defense Company, and Art Schoeni (USN Retired). My thanks is also extended to Bill Halsey for his professional copy camera work and to my wife,
Linda Sullivan for her help in proofreading. In addition, the following people
and organizations have made material available for this book:

Hal Andrews	LTV Aerospace and Defense Co
Roger Besecker	Bob Lawson
Paul Bower	Don Linn
Peter Bowers	Peter Mancus
Robert Carlisle	Paul McDaniel
Bill Curry	Hideki Nagakubo
Dr Carlton Eddy	Sqn Leader Peter Russell-Smith
Bob Esposito	Art Schoeni
W F Gemeinhardt	Larry Smalley
Bill Halsey	Don Spering/A.I.R.
Tom Jackson	Al Ueckert, Jr
Clay Jansson	US Navy
Duane Kasulaka	USMC
Bill Larkins	

(Right) F-8J (149195) of VF-51 launches from the port catapult of BON HOMME RICHARD
(CVA-31) operating in the Gulf of Tonkin off the coast of Vietnam. 13 June 1970 (US Navy
via Bill Curry)

INTRODUCTION

XF8U-1

In 1952, with the arrival of the age of supersonic jet aviation, the US Navy was well aware of its need to move into the supersonic age with carrier based jet aircraft. That the Air Force had its Century Series aircraft coming off the drawing boards and were now beginning take shape, further emphasized the need for a Navy MACH-1 fighter.

In September of 1952, the Navy Department announced its need for a *supersonic day fighter of rugged construction, capable of landing at 100 knots, folding wings, heavy firepower, resistance to open sea weather conditions, and simplicity of maintenance and handling.* Never before had an aircraft carrier based fighter been required to exceed the speed of sound in level flight. Eight different aircraft companies responded to the challenge with proposals and designs. In the end, it would come down to a choice between the Grumman F11F Tigerjet and the Chance Vought XF8U-1 Crusader, with the Chance Vought design eventually winning the contract.

Vought Aircraft had had phenomenal success with its F4U Corsair design during World War Two but had fallen on hard times in trying to make the transition from the piston engine to the jet engine. In the words of Barret Tillman author of *MIG MASTER*, "...none of the F4U's immediate successors even began to live up to the Corsair's reputation. The next three designs were, respectively, a dud, a dead-end, and a disappointment." The "dud" being the unconventional XF5U Flying Flapjack which was cancelled before full flight trials were even begun. The "dead-end" was the F6U Pirate, Vought's first venture into the jet age. The Pirate was under powered and slower than late model F4U's, it was used as a development aircraft and nothing more. While initially a very promising design, "the disaointment", the F7U Cutlass, was slow and difficult to fly. Nicknamed 'Gutless', the F7U was terminated after some 330 examples were built. When Chance Vought, then a division of United Aircraft Corporation, submitted its XF8U design in response to the Navy's Mach One requirement the Dallas based aircraft manufacturer, after three losers in a row, was in a *must-win* situation.

In light of its previous design submissions Vought was expected to submit a radical design. Instead, however, Vought submitted a conventional design enhanced by state-of-the-art technology. Vought opted for a 42 degree swept wing that was hinged at the rear, allowing a two position variable incidence.

In June of 1953, Chance Vought Aircraft received BuAer approval to build two XF8U-1 prototypes (138899/138900). The Vought division broke away from United Aircraft Corporation and began to operating independently as Vought Aircraft with the success or failure of the company hinging on the success or failure of the unflown XF8U-1 design, now named Crusader. The move from United Aircraft Corporation by Vought proved to be most fortuitous with the Crusader becoming a reality only twenty-one months after the XF8U proposal was accepted by BuAer. In March of 1955 the XF8U-1 prototype (138899) Crusader was loaded on board an Air Force C-124 Globemaster and flown to Edwards Air Force Base where on 25 March the Crusader was flown for the first time with Vought chief test pilot John Konrad at the controls. The flight lasted for just under an hour and firmly established the US Navy in the supersonic carrier aviation business by becoming the first shipboard aircraft to exceed MACH 1 in level flight. The Crusader did the unheard of, it flew supersonic on its maiden flight. The XF8U-1 was powered by a single Pratt and Whitney J57-P4 jet engine that delivered 10,200 pounds of dry thrust and 13,200 pounds with afterburner, the same engine that powered the Crusader's closest contemporary, the Air Force's F-100 Super Sabre. A Marquardt Ram Air Turbine (RAT) was provided for emergency power. The RAT could be deployed from the starboard fuselage section at up to 725 knots to generate auxiliary electrical and hydraulic power.

The most unique feature of the XF8U-1 was the variable incidence wing. This variable incidence, allowing the wing to be raised seven degrees, was accomplished hydraulically by a single piston mounted in the forward starboard fuselage center section, allowing the en-

Chance Vought's Chief Test Pilot, John W Konrad, lands the XF8U-1 prototype 1 (138899) on the Muroc dry lake bed at Edwards AFB, CA after completing the first test flight of the Crusader. Konrad went supersonic during level flight in XF8U-1 during his fifty-two minute test flight on the morning of 25 March 1955. Serving as chase plane was Air Force TF-86F (53-1228). (Chance Vought via Hal Andrews)

tire wing to act as a giant flap by increasing the angle of attack by seven degrees. The rear spar was hinged and used as a pivot point. When the wing was in the down position during level flight it permitted supersonic speed to be easily attained. When raised into the up position it provided additional lift during take-off and allowed a landing speed of just over 100 knots for carrier operation. The high angle of attack provided by the variable incidence wing while in the up position afforded excellent visibility to the pilot during take-offs and landings by keeping the fuselage in a more level position relative to the deck. The Crusader's top mounted wing also allowed the fighter a deeper fuselage design, low to the ground which made possible the use of a shorter, and much lighter landing gear. This arrangement provided much easier access and maintenance. The large fuselage cavity beneath the one-piece wing installation made available space for additional jet fuel to obtain maximum range. The total fuel capacity of the XF8U-1 was 1,165 imperial gallons which allowed about three hours of flying time.

Other engineering innovations built into the Crusader included the interconnection of the ailerons and flaps with the entire leading edge of the wingspan. This installation, along with the variable incidence wing, changed the wing camber and effectively reduced approach speeds for ideal carrier landing conditions. The forty-two degree sweep to the wing provided 350 square feet, the largest wing area of any jet fighter of its time. The outer wing panels were hinged to hydraulically fold and unfold for carrier operations. The wing design was so efficient that there have been seven known instances of F8U Crusaders taking-off, flying and landing while the wing outer panels were in the *folded* position.... and while not a recommended flight procedure, it did tend to confirm the integrity of the design. Chance Vought's Chief engineer J R Clark was quoted as saying that the variable incidence wing was the best way to resolve the problem of the landing approach with a sweptwing aircraft.

Vought provided the XF8U-1 with an all-flying metal tail designed with positive dihedral; the rear portion of the fuselage surrounding the afterburner section of the engine was would allow clearance for the rockets to fire. It was such a close fit that the speed brake had to be partially deployed in order to have clearance for the rocket drawer to open. One of the problems incurred with this rocket drawer installation was the rocket fins coming loose during firing and being ingested into the engine with disastrous results. Besides which, the "Mighty Mouse" rockets proved somewhat less than desirable in terms of accuracy (they went everywhere). The Navy and Vought decided to permanently seal the rocket drawers and they were never used operationally with the Fleet.

The XF8U-1 had a wing span of 35 feet 8 inches and was 54 feet 3 inches long with a height of 15 feet 9 inches at the tail. When a Crusader was in the landing configuration (wing up), the ailerons, flaps and the entire leading edge of the wing span dropped twenty degrees respectively for maximum efficiency during landing and take-off. The cockpit with a manually operated canopy was positioned far forward on the fuselage for maximum visibility. The XF8U-1 Crusader had a gross take-off weight of 27,000 pounds.

Carrier trials were carried out aboard FORRESTAL and BON HOMME RICHARD, with excellent results on both size carriers. The Crusader was ready for production and Fleet service. It was a winner, it was the first operational carrier based fighter to attain a speed in excess of 1,000 mph, it earned the Collier Trophy for design and development, it won the Thompson Trophy for speed, and it was given the first Bureau of Aeronautics Certificate of Merit ever awarded. Before series production ended, Vought would produce 1,261 Crusaders.

Prototype 2, XF8U-1 (138900) is towed down the ramp at Vought's factory in Dallas. The cockpit boarding steps are in the open position. Tail markings are Red, Black and White. 1955 (Chance Vought via Hal Andrews)

Prototype 1, XF8U-1 (138899) with the variable incidence wing in the up position. The wing leading edges are deflected along with the flaps to give maximum lift to the wing. Markings are Red outlined in White. 28 May 1956 (US Navy via Hal Andrews)

constructed of Titanium for lighter weight and resistance to the high temperatures in that area. Over 650 pounds of Titanium was used in the wing structure and rear fuselage section. For additional weight savings, the electrical system was all Alternating Current rather than the usual dual Alternating Current/Direct Current combination.

The flight controls were provided with three independent control systems for maximum protection from battle damage. For escape from a terminally damaged aircraft, Vought provided the pilot with a piston cannon powered ejection seat. A Vought adaptation of the Douglas A-4 Skyhawk ejection seat, it was operated by a two-stage face curtain. When activated, the piston kicked the ejection seat, and the pilot, approximately 150 feet up and out of the cockpit with automatic seat separation and parachute release. While not recommended for zero/zero use, the ejection seat could safely be used at low altitudes.

The streamlined XF8U-1 had a rearward retracting nosewheel and a pair of forward retracting main gear. The arresting hook was fully retractable into the rear underside of the fuselage. Armament for the Crusader was four fixed-position, forward-firing 20MM MK-12 Colt cannons with 144 rounds per gun. This firepower was supplemented by a forward-firing rocket pack located in the underside of the fuselage just aft of the nosewheel installation and forward of the speedbrake. Thirty-two 2.75 inch 'Mighty Mouse' folding-fin rockets were honeycombed into the rocket pack. Plans called for the rear-hinged compartment to drop approximately nine inches at the forward end which

F8U Development

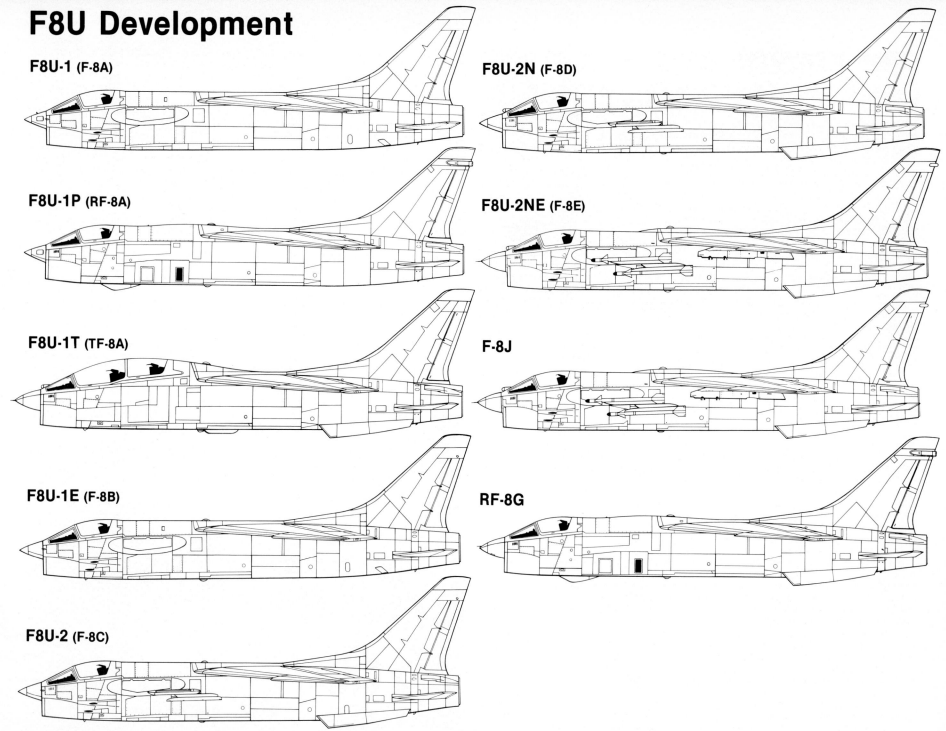

F8U-1 (F-8A)

F8U-1P (RF-8A)

F8U-1T (TF-8A)

F8U-1E (F-8B)

F8U-2 (F-8C)

F8U-2N (F-8D)

F8U-2NE (F-8E)

F-8J

RF-8G

F8U-1 (F-8A)

With few changes from the prototype, the Chance Vought **F8U-1** Crusader began to roll off the Dallas assembly line, with the first production aircraft flying on 30 September of 1955 only some twenty-seven months after the contract was awarded to Vought and only Six months after the prototype flew for the first time. After the first thirty F8U-1 Crusaders produced the Pratt and Whitney J57-P-12 engine was replaced with the more powerful Pratt and Whitney J57-P-4A engine providing a dry thrust of 10,900 pounds and 16,600 pounds in afterburner. The original thirty F8U-1 aircraft were later retrofitted with the more powerful engine. The new engine allowed the Crusader to operate at altitudes near 50,000 feet and at speeds in excess of MACH 1.5.

The fuselage mounted 20MM cannon armament was supplemented by single rocket launch racks mounted on each side of the fuselage just in front of and below the wing that was capable of handling heat-seeking Sidewinder missiles. The rocket drawer concept was retained, but it remained unused and was normally sealed shut.

The Vought ejection seat, was soon replaced by the more efficient fully automatic Martin-Baker F5 seat.

In September of 1955 the Navy ordered the installation of *probe* type inflight refueling equipment on its fighter and attack aircraft. After the fiftieth production aircraft the F8U-1 had refueling capability built into it with the early -1s being retrofitted with refueling probes. The refueling probe was installed on the port side of the fuselage just aft and below the cockpit canopy and was covered by a streamlined elliptical fairing. The refueling probe folded outward and into the windstream during refueling operations.

A unique concept was considered and presented to the Air Force in mock-up. The Optimum Survival Containment And Rescue Capsule (OSCAR), called for the part of the fuselage from the canopy bulkhead forward to separate from the remainder of the aircraft as a capsule which contained large parachutes to bring the module safely to the surface from any altitude down to twenty-five feet underwater. This revolutionary concept was not implemented in the Crusader series.

After carrier qualifications aboard FORRESTAL in April of 1956, F8U-1s began to come off the assembly line at the rate of eight per month. After Fleet indoctrination, VF-32 stationed at NAS Cecil Field, FL was the first East Coast squadron to receive the new fighter in March of 1957. Such was the Navy's confidence in their Crusader that new aircraft began to be delivered directly to operational squadrons without going through an intermediate inspection and testing unit. On the West Coast, VF-154 and VF(AW)-3 were first to be equip, with VF-211, 142, 143, VFP-61, and USMC squadrons VMF-122, 225, 312, 333 and 334 following as aircraft became available. The Crusader quickly and firmly established itself as the Navy's premier fighter. In January of 1962, VMF(AW)-451 (The Warlords), became the first squadron to make a *non-stop* trans-Pacific deployment when it flew from MCAS El Toro, CA to Atsugi, Japan. This was accomplished with inflight refueling being provided by several squadrons of AJ-1 Savage tankers.

A number of records were broken by the F8U-1 Crusader, the most notable of which was *Project One Grand* (the attempt to break the 1,000 mph mark). On the morning of 21 August 1956, Cdr R W 'Duke' Windsor took off from NOTS ChinaLake, CA flying F8U-1 (141345) on a speed run. His aim was to break the existing record of 822 mph set by an Air Force F-100C Super Sabre. After two passes through the measured course, the F8U-1 Crusader was clocked at an incredible average speed of 1,015 mph, earning it the highly prized Thompson trophy.

During 1961, F8U-1 production was completed and in late 1962 when the Department of Defense changed the existing system of aircraft designations the F8U-1 became the F-8A.

In 1964, VF-701/703 and VMF-111/112, Naval Reserve units, began receiving F-8As (F8U-1's) at NAS Dallas. No less than twenty reserve squadrons would eventually fly the F-8A Crusader before the fighter was withdrawn from service.

F8U-1 (140444), the first production Crusader, was the world's fastest Naval fighter. The full-span wing leading edge is slightly deflected and the 20MM cannon openings are faired over. The trim color is Black with a Red outline and the nose carries a test probe installation. September 1955 (Chance Vought via Hal Andrews)

F8U-1 (140446), the third production Crusader during carrier suitability tests is being towed forward on the flight deck of FORRESTAL (CVA-59). The variable incidence wing is in the up position, the leading edges are deflected downward twenty-five degrees, and the wing is folded at mid-span. 4 April 1956 (US Navy via Hal Andrews)

F8U-1 (141363) production 33 on the final assembly line. The Vought ejection seat is in the foreground and the 'Mighty Mouse' 2.75 inch rocket drawer is under the starboard wing. Dallas, 1956 (LTV Aerospace)

F8U-1 (141345) broke the existing world speed record on 21 August 1956. Flown by Cdr R W Windsor Jr, the Crusader was clocked at an average speed of 1,015 mph over a fifteen kilometer course at NOTS China Lake, CA. (via Pete Bowers)

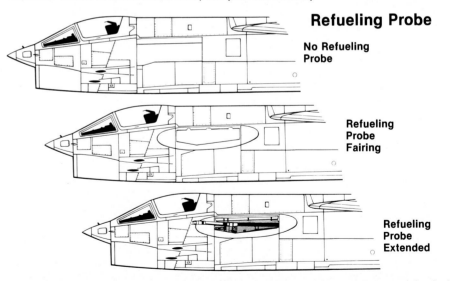

Refueling Probe

No Refueling Probe

Refueling Probe Fairing

Refueling Probe Extended

(Left) With its refueling probe extended, F8U-1 (143706) of VX-3 prepares to take fuel aboard. Refueling equipment was added to the fiftieth production aircraft and retrofitted to earlier production aircraft. The circular fuselage intakes over the flying tail provided for afterburner cooling. 1956 (Chance Vought via Hal Andrews)

F8U-1 (142409) of VFAW-3 is seen at an Armed Forces Day open house at NAS Moffett Field, CA. The rocket-drawer is deployed in the 'open' position along with the partially opened dive brake. VFAW-3 was one of the first West Coast squadrons to be equipped with the Crusader. 18 May 1957 (Bill Larkins)

F8U-1 (143735), 'all down and dirty', prepares to recover aboard HANCOCK (CVA-19). Colorful International Orange markings identified the Crusaders of VF-154. The Black and White striped arresting hook, seen fully extended, retracted flush into the fuselage. 22 November 1957 (US Navy via Hal Andrews)

Variable Incidence Wing

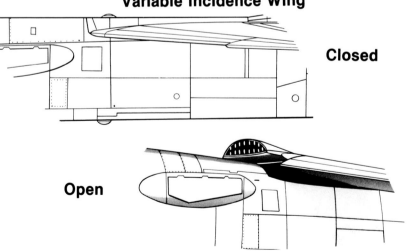

Closed

Open

(Right) F8U-1 (143683) of VF-211 has Red markings on the fuselage, and Red and White checkerboard on the vertical stabilizer. The jet intake has been secured against foreign object damage (FOD). NAS Miramar, CA. 10 August 1957 (Larry Smalley)

F8U-1 (145413) of VMF-334 landing at MCAAS Yuma, AZ. The inboard section of the starboard leading edge shows a heavily-weathered condition. VMF-334 was stationed at MCAS El Toro, CA. 2 December 1959 (USMC via Hal Andrews)

(Below) Securing a hatch aft of the open canopy, this Naval officer makes F8U-1 (145348) of VX-3 ready to get underway after an unscheduled stop at Wilmington, NC. 1959. (Paul J McDaniel)

F8U-1 (145357) of VF-11 broke the starboard landing gear strut while coming aboard FRANKLIN D ROOSEVELT (CVA-42). Dragging the flight deck, the Magnesium strut flamed instantly. Lt (jg) Kryway punched out in his Martin-Baker ejection seat. He was picked up by a helicopter almost immediately after landing in the sea. The Crusader went 'deep-six'. 21 October 1961 (US Navy via Robert Carlisle)

Ram Air Turbine (RAT)

Vought Ejection Seat

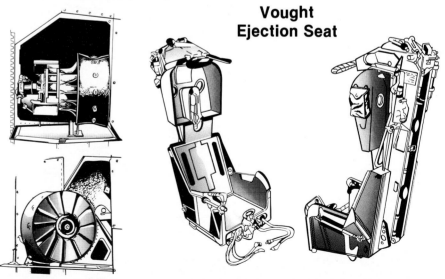

(Right) F8U-1 Crusaders (143743, 144457, 145320 and 145363) with hooks down pass abeam HANCOCK (CVA-19) to break for landing. VF-211 used Red and White checkerboard trim on their rudders, lettering was Black. Missile racks aft of the National insignia handled a heat-seeking Sidewinder missile. 1960 (US Navy via Bill Curry)

F8U-1 (F-8A)

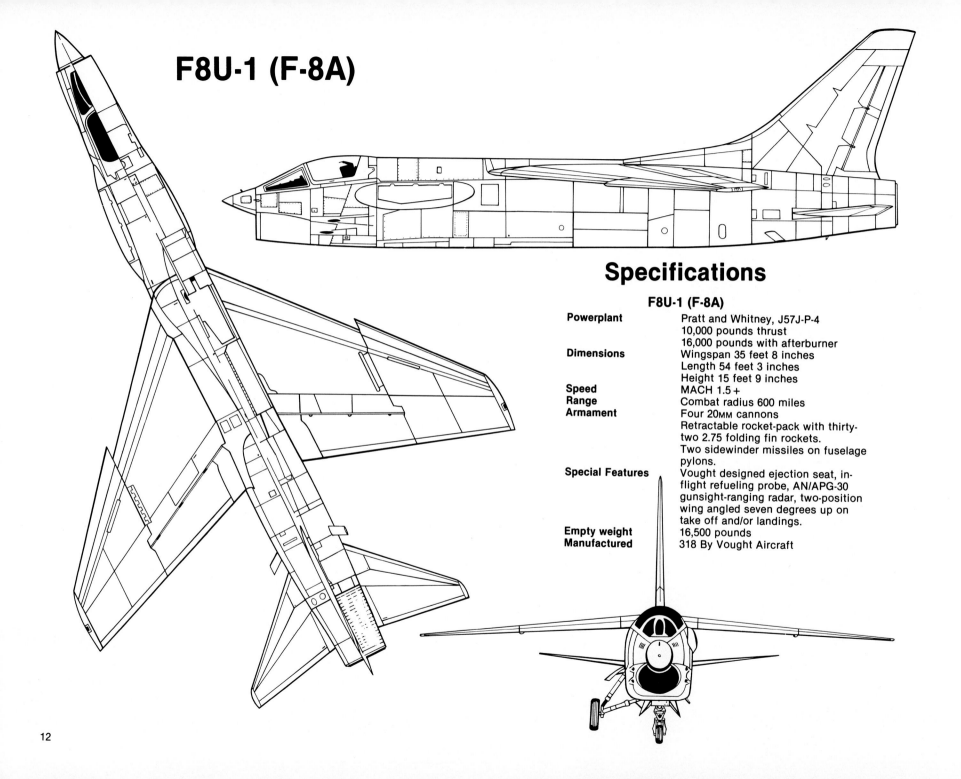

Specifications

F8U-1 (F-8A)

Powerplant	Pratt and Whitney, J57J-P-4 10,000 pounds thrust 16,000 pounds with afterburner
Dimensions	Wingspan 35 feet 8 inches Length 54 feet 3 inches Height 15 feet 9 inches
Speed	MACH 1.5 +
Range	Combat radius 600 miles
Armament	Four 20MM cannons Retractable rocket-pack with thirty-two 2.75 folding fin rockets. Two sidewinder missiles on fuselage pylons.
Special Features	Vought designed ejection seat, in-flight refueling probe, AN/APG-30 gunsight-ranging radar, two-position wing angled seven degrees up on take off and/or landings.
Empty weight	16,500 pounds
Manufactured	318 By Vought Aircraft

F8U-1 (143748) of VMF-122, the first USMC squadron to receive Crusaders, seen at MCAS Yuma, AZ. The smoke stained portion of the nose section of the fuselage resulted from firing the 20mm cannons. Markings are Blue and White with a Red cross on the White shield. March 1960 (Bill Swisher via Clay Jansson)

Missile Launch Rack

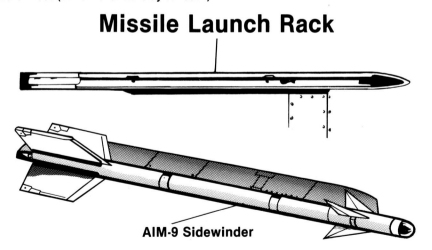

AIM-9 Sidewinder

F8U-1 (145322) of VF-103 'The Sluggers' flies over coastal Virginia near NAS OCEANA. The squadron insignia is aft of the canopy. The trim colors are Yellow outlined in Black and the fuselage is painted completely, even over the afterburner area. C.1960 (US Navy via Hal Andrews)

The 'Death Rattlers' of VMF-323 flew this F8U-1 (143679), the rocket launching rails have been removed. Five Maroon colored diamonds are located high on the tail. 30 January 1960 (Clay Jansson)

F8U-1 Crusaders (144429 and 144431) of VF-62 over NAS Cecil Field, Fl. The placement of the aircraft number on the afterburner section was rarely seen. Trim colors are Yellow and Black. 1960 (US Navy via Hal Andrews)

F8U-1 (143793) of VX-4 is rigged for target towing. Red target is let out behind the tow plane via a wire from the self-powered pod on the port fuselage that handles both the deployment and retrieval of the gunnery target. PMTC Pt Mugu, CA. 19 May 1962 (Doug Olsen via Clay Jansson)

F-8A (F8U-1) (144431) of VF-62 is towed forward on the flight deck of ENTERPRISE (CVAN-65). All flying control surfaces, including the 'flying tail' are painted White. The streamline of the upper fuselage can be seen to good advantage. The trim color markings are Yellow and Black. 1967 (Art Schoeni)

F-8A (F8U-1) (142409) of VMF-312 'Checkerboards' is parked on the ramp at MCAS Beaufort, SC. The burned effect on the paint on the exhaust section comes from the tremendous heat generated by the Pratt and Whitney J57-P-4A's afterburner. Tail markings are Black and White checkerboard bordered with a Yellow stripe at the top and a Red one at the bottom. The shark mouth on the nose has a checkerboard instead of teeth. 1966 (WF Gemeinhardt)

An F-8A (F8U-1) of VMF(AW)-235 on its final approach at NAF Atsugi, Japan. The writing on the wing center section bulkhead reads SIXTH FLEET. Markings are White stars on a Red field outlined in White. August 1968 (Author's Collection)

DF-8F

During 1968 plans called for forty F-8A (F8U-1) airframes to be modified to F-8M standards but due to a lack of airframe availability, no F-8Ms were in fact produced. However, some F-8As were modified into the drone-controller configuration under the designation DF-8F.

(Below) Colorful Orange and Black markings identify this DF-8F (145319) of VC-7 'TALLEYHOERS' seen at its home-station, NAS Miramar, CA. This was one of a number of F-8A Crusaders converted to DF-8F Drone Controllers. The blade antennas on the fuselage spine just aft of the cockpit, on the belly just aft of the nose wheel, and on the lower port rear fuselage in front of the stabilator were unique to the DF-8F variant. 19 February 1966 (Clay Jansson)

(Below) DF-8F (143793) of VC-5 during its final approach at the Naval Air Station at Atsugi, Japan. Modex is 'UE' in Black, outlined in White on an Orange and Red checkerboard. The 20MM cannon armament was maintained on the Drone Controller variant. 1970 (Hideki Nagakubo)

This DF-8F (144456) Crusader of VC-8 is one of the more colorfully marked Drone Controllers in a Glossy Sea Blue and Yellow paint scheme. These high-visibility markings were to make sure that the pilots practicing gunnery would shoot at the Drone and not at the Drone Controller. NAS Brooklyn, NY. 4 June 1967 (Clay Jansson)

F8U-1E (F-8B)

After 315 F8U-1 Crusader day fighters had been produced, the **F8U-1E** replaced it on the assembly line. Essentially the same as the F8U-1, the F8U-1E was equipped with the AN/APS-67 radar scanner in the nose replacing the APG-30 fire control system, and providing the F8U-1E with limited all-weather capability. The F8U-1E prototype, a converted F8U-1 (145318), flew on 3 September 1958. Armament remained at four 20MM Colt cannons and two sidewinders, and although the rocket drawer was retained, it remained sealed. The F8U-1E was capable of speeds in excess of 880 knots, had a service ceiling of 42,000 feet, and a combat radius of 345 nautical miles. One hundred thirty F8U-1Es were produced. In 1962 under DOD's redesignation order the F8U-1E was redesignated to the F-8B.

(Below) F8U-1E (145540) in factory-fresh finish. VMF-312 markings have been carefully applied. The clear section on the bottom of the nose cone is for the gun camera. The leading edges of the wings and stabilator are unpainted. 1959 (USMC via Hal Andrews)

(Above) F8U-1E (145454) of VF-32 cruises off the coast of Virginia Beach, VA near its home base of NAS Oceana. This Crusader was assigned to Carrier Air Wing Three aboard SARATOGA (CVA-60). Fuselage mounted Sidewinder missile racks are carried which overlap the National Insignia. Trim color on the tail is Yellow. C.1960 (U.S. Navy via Bill Curry)

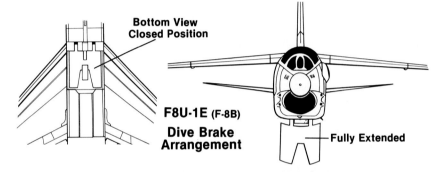

Bottom View
Closed Position

F8U-1E (F-8B)
Dive Brake
Arrangement

Fully Extended

(Below) F8U-1E (145517) of VF-33 is tied down aboard INDEPENDENCE (CVA-62). Trim markings are Yellow outlined in Black, rudder is overall Yellow with Black stars and tip. A Black lightning bolt is carried on Yellow wingtips, and a Yellow lightning bolt outlined in Black is carried on the fuselage under the wing. All Fleet Crusader fighters were painted in the Gull Gray over Glossy White paint scheme. C. 1960 (via Pete Bowers)

16

F-8L

In December of 1968 Vought began modification of the F-8B (F8U-1E) Crusader under a remanufacturing program designed to extend the service life of the Crusader. The prototype was F-8B (145318). This remanufactured variant was designated **F-8L**, and had instrument changes and cockpit modifications that brought about a increase in night flying capabilities. New catapult keels were installed where necessary and approach power compensators were installed to assist in carrier landings. While ventral fins were not installed, provisions were made for them with attachment points, however, they were faired over with diamond shaped fairings. Sixty-one F-8Bs were rebuilt as F-8Ls.

(Above) Heavy smoke stains from cannon gunfire shows on the nose of F8U-1E (145442) of VF-124. This unit Fleet-qualified Naval Aviators on the Crusader for West Coast squadrons. The colorful Orange markings on the tail have Black trim with White outlines. Jet inlet and outlet openings have been sealed against FOD. NAS Miramar, CA. C.1961 (David Lucabaugh via Don Linn)

F8U-1E (145466) of VF-154 flies low over the flight deck after being waved off CORAL SEA (CVA-43). All Douglas built products (A-1, A-3 and A-4) line the flight deck. 4 March 1961 (US Navy via Hal Andrews)

(Below) F-8B (F8U-1E) (145453) flown by the Naval Air Reserve Training Unit and the Marine Reserves attached to NAS Willow Grove, PA. Dual names were allowed on reserve aircraft when flown by both Navy and Marine reserve pilots. 8 May 1968 (US Navy via Bill Curry)

F8U-1P (RF-8A)

To fill a need for a fast high flying photo reconnaissance aircraft Vought developed the photo Crusader under the designation **F8U-1P**. The prototype for the photo Crusader was F8U-1 BuNo 141363. The F8U-1P, while identical to the standard F8U-1 from the wing back, had a completely re-designed nose section. All armament and fire control systems were removed and in their place Vought installed cameras: three trimetrogen cameras, two vertical and one forward facing, and provisions for the storage and release of photo-flash bombs for night photography. The forward under surface was flattened, and the refueling probe was made flush with and completely enclosed in the fuselage, creating a square, flat-sided forward fuselage which called for some area-rule treatment for the fuselage via a hump over the forward part of the wing extending to the rear of the canopy. Because the Recce pilot depended on speed rather than air combat maneuvering (ACM) the stabilizer was decreased in size. The thirty-second production F8U-1 was used as the F8U-1P prototype which flew for the first time on 17 December 1957, with final deliveries being made in early 1960 after 144 F8U-1Ps were built.

In July of 1957, Major John Glenn flying F8U-1P (144608) set the transcontinental speed record flying from Los Angeles, CA to New York City in three hours twenty-three minutes averaging a speed of 726 mph. The F8U-1P was redesignated to **RF-8A** in 1962.

During the Cuban Missile Crisis in 1962, RF-8A (F8U-1P) Crusaders flown by pilots of VFP-62 and VMCJ-2 confirmed the presence of Soviet missiles and their locations. From that time until their eventual removal, photo-Crusaders recorded the progress of the situation.

F8U-1P (145637) of VMCJ-1 lands on the steel-planked runway at Taiwan, Formosa during OPERATION BLUESTAR. The tail hook is deployed to catch the MOREST gear for an arrested landing. 27 March 1960 (USMC via Hal Andrews)

F8U-1P (145635) of VMCJ-2 is seen just off the Atlantic Coast near its home base, MCAS Cherry Point. The forward nose section has been painted White. Vents on the fuselage aft of the National insignia are for cooling electronic equipment. April 1959 (USMC via Bill Curry)

F8U-1P (144622) of VFP-62 was the seventeenth photo Crusader built. The various camera windows on the side and bottom of the fuselage can be seen. 1961 (US Navy via Hal Andrews)

RF-8A (F8U-1P) (145622) of VFP-62 was one of five Crusaders modified with ventral fins and F-8E type wings with pylons to carry ECM pods. This aircraft participated in photo runs across Cuba during the missile crisis of 1962. (Chance Vought via Hal Andrews)

F8U-1

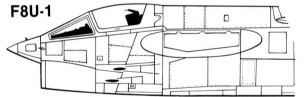

F8U-1P

F8U-1

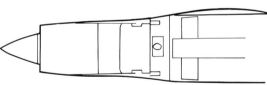

F8U-1P

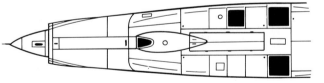

F8U-1 **F8U-1P**

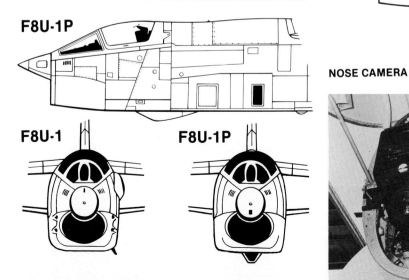

NOSE CAMERA

PORT AFT BAY

STARBOARD BAY

(Above) RF-8A (145608) of VFP-62 is attached to Carrier Air Wing One aboard FRANKLIN D ROOSEVELT (CVA-42). The rear portion of the fuselage covering the afterburner section of the Pratt and Whitney J57-P-4 is unpainted. The trim color on the tail is White on Blue. A Pluto emblem is carried on the fuselage under the wing. 7 June 1964 (US Navy via Bill Curry)

The area-rule (curve) design changes to the upper portion of the fuselage forward of the wing can be seen on this RF-8A (146837) of VFP-63, Charlie Detachment from KITTY HAWK (CVA-63). From the wing aft, the photo-Crusader was identical to the F8U-1 (F-8A). 1965 (US Navy via Bill Curry)

RF-8A (146889) of VFP-62 with rather elaborate markings, some of which are the results of having crossed the Equator. The name stencilled on the canopy is "LCDR Gig Coraughton SHELLBACK". ENTERPRISE (CVAN-65). 1964 (Art Schoeni)

F8U-2 (F-8C)

On 20 August 1957 the F8U-2 prototype (F8U-1 BuNo 140477), powered by a Pratt and Whitney J-57-P-16 engine that delivered 13,000 pounds of static thrust and 17,500 pounds in afterburner, flew for the first time. This more powerful installation resulted in a faster Crusader capable of 960 knots with a service ceiling of 41,000 feet and a combat radius of 320 nautical miles. To assist in cooling the tremendous heat generated by the afterburner, Vought added two cooling intakes to the rear fuselage on top of the afterburner cone. To solve a yawing problem that had been plaguing the Crusader at high altitudes, low aspect ratio ventral stabilizing fins were installed on the lower rear fuselage. Introduced on the F8U-2 were 'Y' type missile racks that permitted the installation of four Sidewinder missiles (two on each rack). F8U-2's had improved radar and fire control capability.

The first production F8U-2 flew on 20 August 1958 with Jim Omvig at the controls. It possessed a rate-of-climb of 16,500 feet-per-minute with a maximum speed of MACH 1.7, and was flown very close to MACH 2 during the test program. This version of the Crusader was delivered with factory installed Martin-Baker low level ejection seats. First deliveries of the F8U-2 Crusader was to VF-84 at NAS Oceana, VA on 4 April 1959. During the 1958 mid-East crisis in Lebanon, the F8U-2 flew operations in July and August from the 6th Fleet carriers SARATOGA AND ESSEX. In 1962 the F8U-2 was redesignated to F-8C.

F-8C (F8U-2) Crusaders were flown in combat in Vietnam by both the Navy and Marine Corps, where Navy F-8Cs scored six kills by downing five MiG-17s and one MiG-21.

The fourth production F8U-1 (140447) served as the prototype for the F8U-2 Crusader. Revised external features included the addition of ventral fins and airscoops mounted on the aft fuselage for afterburner cooling. The F8U-2 was powered by a J57-P-16 Pratt and Whitney engine. Dallas, TX. 1958 (Chance Vought via Hal Andrews)

F8U-2 (145559) of VF-84, the first squadron to receive the more-powerful Crusader. The air-to-air refueling probe has been extended and attached to a refueling line. Just aft of the nosewheel doors the rocket-drawer can be seen in the open position. NAF Washington, DC May of 1959 (Sqn Leader Russell-Smith)

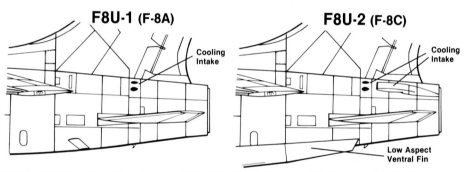

F8U-1 (F-8A)   **F8U-2 (F-8C)**

Cooling Intake

Cooling Intake

Low Aspect Ventral Fin

F8U-2 (146939) of East-Coast based VMF-451 at NAS Miramar, CA. The variable incidence wing has been secured in the takeoff/landing position. Trim color is Dark Blue with White stars on the fin, wing tips and ventral fins. 1959 (via Pete Bowers)

(Above) F8U-2 (147008) of VF-91 carries a Sidewinder on the single port missile rack. The ventral fins and afterburner cooling scoops introduced on this version became standard equipment on all subsequent versions of the Crusader. San Francisco, CA. 18 September 1960 (Larry Smalley)

(Below) First production F8U-2 (145546) is seen during carrier qualifications aboard SHANGRI LA (CVA-38) in November of 1966. The Naval Air Test Center (NATC) markings on the Red and Orange tail are White with a Black outline. (Art Schoeni)

(Left) F8U-2 (145567) of VF-142, also carrying the single missile rail, in flight near NAS Miramar, CA. 13 February 1961 (US Navy via Hal Andrews)

F-8C (F8U-2) (146969) of VMF-334 parked on the ramp near the Operations Building at NAS Alameda, CA. The nose gear is in the fully-extended position. 20 May 1967 (Larry Smalley)

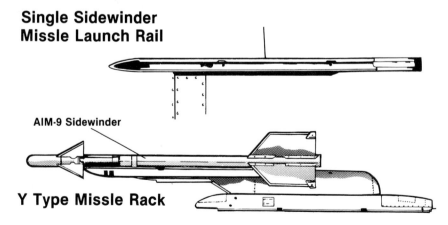

Single Sidewinder Missle Launch Rail

AIM-9 Sidewinder

Y Type Missle Rack

F-8C (146996) of VF-24 carries four MiG kills on the ventral fin, applied for the MiGs destroyed by the squadron in combat over Vietnam. The new 'Y' missile rack capable of handling a pair of sidewinders obscures a great deal of the National Insignia. A small ECM antenna housing is mounted just above the rudder. NAS Dallas, TX. July 1968 (Authors Collection)

F-8C (F8U-2) (145550) of VMF-321, Marine Reserves, lands at MCAS Cherry Point, NC. The trailing edge of the vertical tail has a small ECM antenna housing just above the rudder. 13 April 1971 (Jim Sullivan)

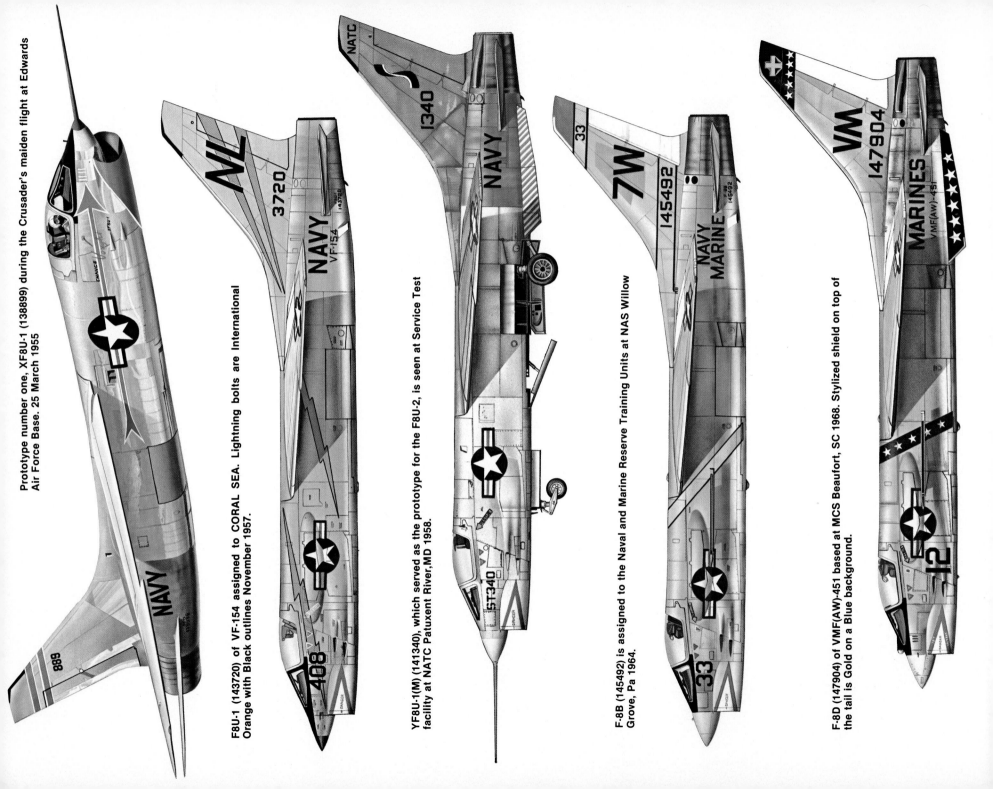

Prototype number one, XF8U-1 (138899) during the Crusader's maiden flight at Edwards Air Force Base. 25 March 1955

F8U-1 (143720) of VF-154 assigned to CORAL SEA. Lightning bolts are International Orange with Black outlines November 1957.

YF8U-1(M) (141340), which served as the prototype for the F8U-2, is seen at Service Test facility at NATC Patuxent River,MD 1958.

F-8B (145492) is assigned to the Naval and Marine Reserve Training Units at NAS Willow Grove, Pa 1964.

F-8D (147904) of VMF(AW)-451 based at MCS Beaufort, SC 1968. Stylized shield on top of the tail is Gold on a Blue background.

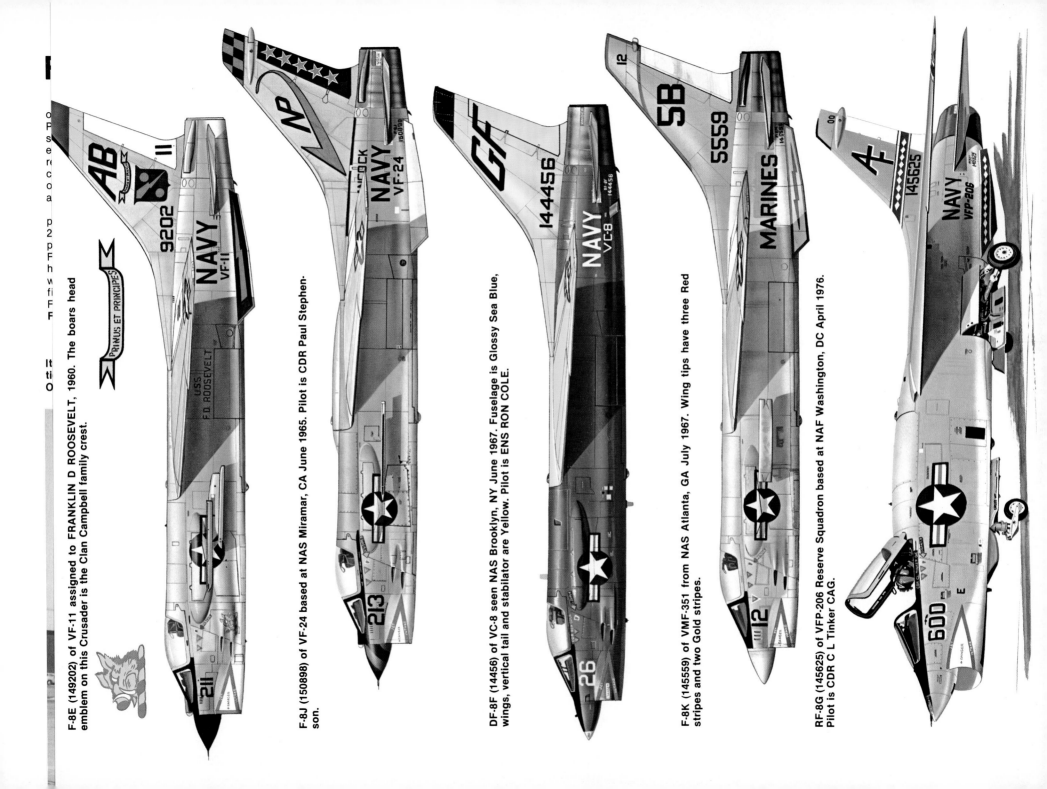

F-8E (149202) of VF-11 assigned to FRANKLIN D ROOSEVELT, 1960. The boars head emblem on this Crusader is the Clan Campbell family crest.

PRIMUS ET PRINCIPES

F-8J (150898) of VF-24 based at NAS Miramar, CA June 1965. Pilot is CDR Paul Stephenson.

DF-8F (14456) of VC-8 seen NAS Brooklyn, NY June 1967. Fuselage is Glossy Sea Blue, wings, vertical tail and stabilator are Yellow. Pilot is ENS RON COLE.

F-8K (145559) of VMF-351 from NAS Atlanta, GA July 1967. Wing tips have three Red stripes and two Gold stripes.

RF-8G (145625) of VFP-206 Reserve Squadron based at NAF Washington, DC April 1976. Pilot is CDR C L Tinker CAG.

F-8D Crusaders (147913, 147923 and 148629) of VF-32 off SARATOGA (CAV-60). The Yellow trim markings have Black outlines. This variant of the Crusader was powered by the 18,000 pound thrust Pratt and Whitney J57-P-20 engine capable of reaching speeds of MACH 1.9. February of 1965 (US Navy via Bill Curry)

F8U-2N
(F-8D)

ECM Fairings

(Left) F-8D (148641) of VF-174, the East Coast training squadron, over NAS Cecil Field, FL. This version had a combat radius of 650 nautical miles and was the first model to be equipped with an infra-red scanner which was mounted just in front of the windscreen. 18 August 1964 (US Navy via Bill Curry)

F-8D (148695) of VMF(AW)-333 on the ramp at MCAS Yuma, AZ. Green and White trim markings were applied to the tail. The multiple 'Y' rack could handle two Sidewinders, doubling the number of missiles the Crusader could carry to four. Vought deleted the rocket pack in favor of added fuel capacity. The infra-red scanner can be seen mounted in front of the windscreen. 11 March 1967 (Clay Jansson)

F8U-2NE (F-8E)

Improving on the F8U-2N variant, Vought produced 286 **F8U-2NE** Crusaders for the Navy. The F8U-2NE prototype flew for the first time on 30 June 1961, and, powered by a Pratt and Whitney J57-P-20A engine, was the fastest Crusader with a maximum speed of 1,120 mph. This variant had a combat radius of 350 nautical miles, a service ceiling of 58,000 feet, and a gross weight of 34,000 pounds. The nose cone was enlarged and rounded to accept the more powerful AN/APQ-94 radar unit with a larger dish that allowed the F8U-2NE to seek out and attack a target at a greater range. The infra-red scanner mounted on the nose that first appeared on the F8U-2N was now standard. An avionics hump on the top of the fuselage containing equipment for firing Bullpup missiles in addition to the standard armament of four Sidewinders and four 20MM cannon. To further increase the versatility of the Crusader, underwing pylons were added which could be used to carry an additional 600 gallons of fuel for extended flight, or carry up to two 2,000 pounds of missiles, rockets, bombs or ECM pods.

Early in 1962 the F8U-2NE completed its carrier trials aboard FORRESTAL and shortly thereafter entered fleet service. The F8U-2NE was redesignated F-8E in late 1962.

During the Vietnam war, a total of ten F-8E (F8U-2NE) Crusaders made confirmed kills accounting for the destruction of eleven MiG-17s and one MiG-21. The story is told of a pair of F-8Es flying from HANCOCK that spotted and pursued a MiG-17. The MiG pilot, realizing that he was under attack, punched out of his aircraft without a shot being fired.

F-8E (150844) of VF-13 off SHANGRI LA (CVA-38) is parked on the ramp at Luga, Malta. The 'Y' type missile racks are installed and the arresting hook is in the down position. Trim color is Dark Blue. May 1965 (Squadron Leader Peter Russell-Smith)

F8U-2N (F-8D)   F8U-2NE (F-8E)

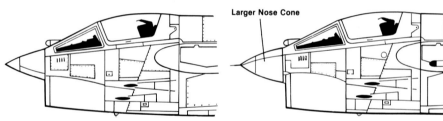

Larger Nose Cone

This F8U-2NE (149218) assigned to the Naval Air Test Center is loaded with eight Zuni rockets and two Bullpup air-to-ground missiles. The installation just aft of the nosewheel is the catapult bridle hookup. 22 October 1962 (US Navy via Hal Andrews)

This F-8E (150326) of VF-91 Satan's Kittens, belongs to Cdr Billy Phillips, of Attack Carrier Air Wing Nineteen from TICONDEROGA (CVA-14). Underwing pylons were added to this version. When not at sea, this colorful Crusader was based at NAS Miramar, CA. 17 September 1966 (Clay Jansson)

F-8E (150907) of VF-111 assigned to ORISKANY (CVA-34) and Carrier Air Wing Sixteen, which had returned from a WestPac tour off Vietnam two months earlier. NAS Miramar, CA. 19 February 1966 (Clay Jansson)

F-8E (150663) of VF-53, assigned to TICONDEROGA (CVA-14) has Yellow with Black outlined trim on the vertical tail and ventral fins. The larger nose radome for the AN/PDQ-94 radar and infra-red scanner installation can be seen to good advantage. NAS Miramar, CA. 16 July 1966 (Clay Jansson)

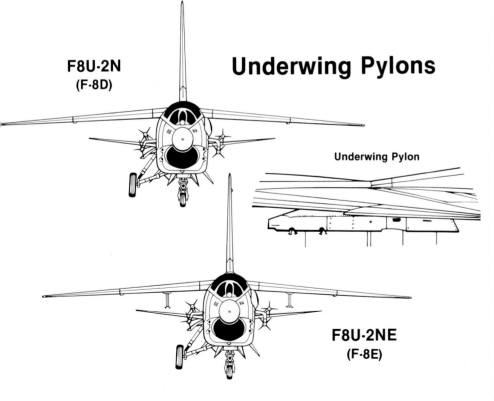

F8U-2N
(F-8D)

Underwing Pylons

Underwing Pylon

F8U-2NE
(F-8E)

F-8E (150670) is flown by Cdr RE Ferguson, the CO of VF-51. The 'Screaming Eagle' insignia can be seen on the Red trimmed tail just over the BuNo. NAS Miramar, CA. 17 September 1966 (Clay Jansson)

F8U-2NE (F-8E)

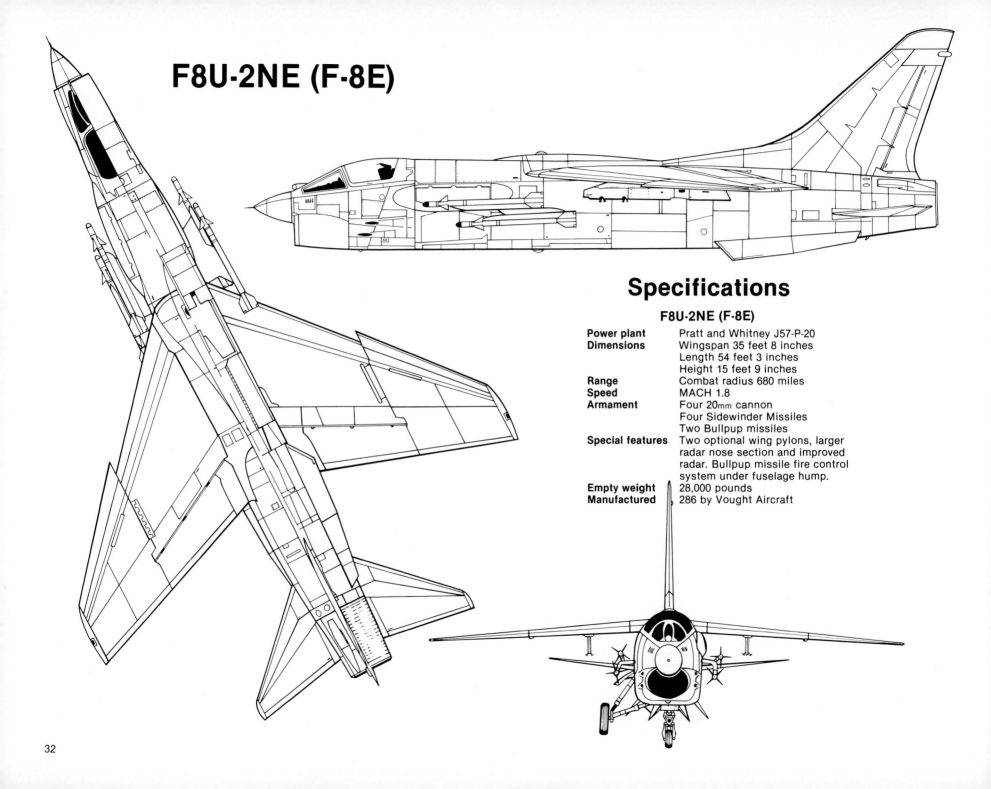

Specifications

F8U-2NE (F-8E)

Power plant	Pratt and Whitney J57-P-20
Dimensions	Wingspan 35 feet 8 inches
	Length 54 feet 3 inches
	Height 15 feet 9 inches
Range	Combat radius 680 miles
Speed	MACH 1.8
Armament	Four 20mm cannon
	Four Sidewinder Missiles
	Two Bullpup missiles
Special features	Two optional wing pylons, larger radar nose section and improved radar. Bullpup missile fire control system under fuselage hump.
Empty weight	28,000 pounds
Manufactured	286 by Vought Aircraft

F-8E (150329) of VMF(AW)-232 'Red Devils' on the ramp at NAS North Island, CA. The nose wheel is at full extension. The USMC flew the Crusader providing close air support during the war in Vietnam. A winged Red Devil carrying a pitch fork on a White diamond outlined in Red is painted on the upper tail. 15 November 1967 (Clay Jansson)

(Below) Returning with its starboard Sidewinder unfired, this F-8E (150666) of VF-53 heads home to BON HOMME RICHARD (CVA-31) over the South China Sea after a strike on North Vietnam. The humid climate and open sea operations wreaked havoc on paint. C.1966 (US Navy via Pete Bowers)

The 'Red Lightnings' of VF-194 from TICONDEROGA (CVA-14) fly F-8Es (150324 and 150932) over the rugged California mountains sharpening their combat skills. This squadron won the Battle Efficiency 'E' which is carried on the forward fuselage. C.1968 (US Navy via Bill Curry)

Parked between missions, with the canopy open, an F-8E (150328) of VMF(AW)-235 is heavily stained from the rigors of combat in Vietnam. The USMC provided close air support with F-8 Crusaders and F-4 Phantoms. Zuni rockets are installed on the lower portion of the 'Y' missile launch rack on this Crusader at Da Nang, Vietnam in September of 1966. (WF Gemeinhardt)

F-8E (150852) of VMF(AW)-333, 'Flying Shamrocks', with trim markings of Green and White. Bombs are carried on the fuselage racks. Cannon smoke stains are seen on the nose section. MCAS Yuma, AZ. 11 March 1967 (Clay Jansson)

F-8E (149150) of VF-211 has the squadron victory total of six MiG kills painted on the ventral fins and has an individual MiG-kill mark beneath the cockpit for its pilot, Cdr Paul Speer, who had downed a MiG-17 over North Vietnam three months earlier. NAS Miramar, CA 27 August 1967 (Clay Jansson)

Well weathered F-8E (149143) flies high above the clouds while returning from a strike on North Vietnam. The open sea conditions during combat operations caused corrosion that quickly deteriorated the paint and showed up every panel line. C.1968 (US Navy via Bill Curry)

F8U-1T (TF-8A)

The seventy-seventh production F8U-1 (14370), having previously been brought up to F8U-2NE standards, was converted into a two-seat trainer by installing a second seat behind the regular seat, and a second full set of controls. In order to increase visibility the second seat was raised 15 inches, and a completely redesigned and enlarged canopy was installed. Power was supplied by a J-57-P-20 engine. Low pressure tires and a drag chute installed for rough field landing The two seater would be the only Crusader to be equipped with a Drag chute. Two of the four 20MM Colt cannons and the rocket pack were removed. Rails to accommodate four Sidewinder missiles were installed on the fuselage sides, and an infra-red scanner was mounted on the nose just forward of the windscreen giving better control of the missiles. Under the designation **F8U-1T** the two seater flew for the first time on 6 February 1962. Although extremely promising the F8U-1T was not put into production due to fiscal cut backs in 1964. Both British and French Military officials showed an interest in the two seater but none were purchased. It was redesignated **TF-8A** in 1962.

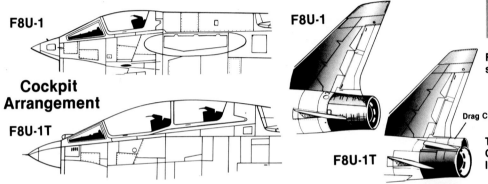

F8U-1

F8U-1

Cockpit Arrangement

F8U-1T

Drag Chute

F8U-1T

F8U-1 (143710) before it was bought up to F8U-1NE standards and modified into a two-seater. 1960 (Chance Vought via Hal Andrews).

The 'TWOSADER' had a completely redesigned canopy and the starboard pair of 20MM Colt cannons were removed and faired over. Brought up to F8U-1NE standards it had a larger nose cone and an infra-red scanner installed on the nose. (Art Schoeni)

(Above) The F8U-1T (143710) taxies forward to launch from INDEPENDENCE. The 'CREWSADER'/'TWOSADER' was assigned to the Flight Test section of NATC Patuxent River, MD. 1967 (US Navy via Hal Andrews)

(Below) Under the redesignation TF-8A, the 'CREWSADER' served with the US Naval Test Pilot School. This was the only version of the Crusader to utilize a drag chute. NATC Patuxent River, MD. 23 April 1973 (Jim Sullivan)

F-8E(FN)

The last production run of Crusaders was a batch of forty-two modified F-8Es built for the French Navy under the designation **F-8E(FN)**. Following the F8U-1T TWOSADER's impressive performance at the Paris Airshow, the French Navy, unable to adapt a domestic manufactured aircraft to the carrier based air superiority role, began to show a great deal of interest in the Vought fighter. The Crusader not only had an impressive performance, and was small enough to operate from French carriers, but its price tag was comparatively low. The only drawback was the 113 knot landing speed of the Crusader which was considered too hot for safe operation on French carriers.

Vought set about reducing the Crusader's landing speed which entailed a great deal of sophisticated modification to the wing. The wing's camber was doubled with a forty degree extension to ailerons and flaps. A Boundary Layer Control (BLC) system was designed in which the engine's high pressure compressor was used to blow air through nozzles mounted in the wing across the flaps and ailerons creating additional airflow and lift at low speeds. This BLC system coupled with full span, double-droop wing leading edges permitted a reduction in landing speed from 113 knots to below 90 knots. The entire tailplane was enlarged for better handling.

The F-8E(FN)'s powerplant was a Pratt and Whitney J57-P-20A which delivered 18,000 pounds of thrust with afterburner, providing a top speed of 943 knots. The 20MM cannon and Sidewinder capability was retained, but the French quickly added the capability of their own ordnance when rails to handle both the Sidewinder and French MATRA 530 were installed on the fuselage. However, flame from the MATRA was found to be damaging the stabilators and six inch leading edges of titanium had to be added to the stabilators.

The prototype for the F-8E(FN) was F-8D BuNo 147036 which carried out the initial flight testing. In April of 1964, 147036 crashed and wing testing had to be successfully carried out by the first French production aircraft. Carrier trials were carried out onboard SHANGRI LA in November of 1964 and shortly thereafter aboard CLEMENCEAU. The F-8E(FN) Crusader was the state-of-the-art Crusader *gunfighter*, and the French Navy would keep it that way, never adding strike capability to it. The original contract called for forty single seat fighters and six TF-8A two seaters plus spares, but when Congress killed production of the two seater, the French order was changed to forty-two single seaters and spares. The last Crusader to roll off the Dallas assembly line was an F8E(FN) delivered in January of 1965. The initial French squadrons equipped with the Crusader were Flotilles 12F and 14F, the same squadrons that years earlier had been equipped with the Vought AU-1 and F4U Corsair.

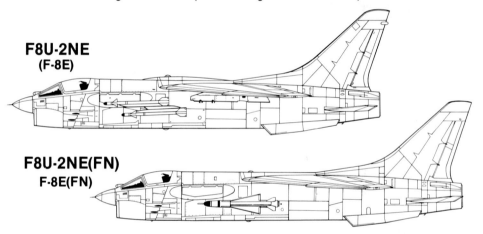

The prototype F-8E(FN) (147036), a re-built F-8D (F8U-2N), is seen landing after its first flight. Multi-National markings appear on this US built fighter manufactured for use by the French Navy (FN). A French Matra missile is carried on the launch rack. This aircraft crashed before testing was finished. (Chance Vought via Hal Andrews)

F8U-2NE
(F-8E)

F8U-2NE(FN)
F-8E(FN)

The first production F-8E(FN) (151732) replaced the crashed prototype (F-8D 147036) and completed the flight test program. The nose has had a test boom installed. This Crusader is armed with only the four 20MM cannon, the missile racks have yet to be installed. June 1964 (Chance Vought via Hal Andrews)

(Above) Chance Vought employees look on as the final Crusader produced, F-8E(FN) (151773) rolls off the assembly line. This was the 'state-of-the-art' Crusader, which would serve as a basis for the remanufactured F-8J series. 25 November 1963 (Chance Vought via Hal Andrews)

(Below) An F-8E(FN) dumps fuel through the wing tip fuel vents. The -FN variant featured a larger tailplane and deeper deflecting flaps. The Pratt and Whitney J57-P-20A engine produced a top speed of 943 knots. Either American made Sidewinder or French made Matra missiles could be carried. 1964 (Chance Vought via Hal Andrews)

F-8E(FN) 2 (151733) lands aboard SHANGRI LA (CVA-38) during carrier trials off the Virginia Coast. This Crusader has just touched-down and is about to pick up a wire. November 1964 (Art Schoeni via Hal Andrews)

REMANUFACTURING

During the mid sixties Vought was designated to begin a program of updating and remanufacturing the F-8 Crusader, breathing new life into the design and extending its service life into the seventies. Load bearing capability was increased, new wings were installed, the arresting gear was improved, the external starter turbine was incorporated internally, the radar was again updated and provisions for ECM and armor protection were added. Ventral fins were added to those aircraft that did not already carry them. Boundary layer control (BLC) and double droop wing leading edges similar to the French variant (F8U-2NE) were installed on the F-8J (updated F-8E). Of the 448 Crusaders remanufactured, the largest number would be the F-8J with 136 being remanufactured during 1968 and 1969.

Original Designation	Number Built	1962 DOD Re-designation	Number Remanufactured	Remanufactured Designation
XF8U-1	2	-	-	-
F8U-1	317	F-8A	-	-
F8U-1P	144	RF-8A	73	RF-8G
F8U-1T	1	TF-8A	-	-
F8U-1E	130	F-8B	63	F-8L
F8U-2	187	F-8C	87	F-8K
F8U-2N	152	F-8D	89	F-8H
F8U-2NE	286	F-8E	136	F-8J
F8U-2FN	42	-	-	-
Total	**1,261**		**448**	

RF-8G

In 1965, remanufacturing was begun to update the RF-8A (F8U-1P) photo Crusader under the designation RF-8G. This was accomplished in two batches, the first fifty-three aircraft were re-built during 1965-67, and a second batch of twenty aircraft during 1968-70, for a total of seventy-three airframes. New features of the RF-8G included multi-position openings for camera installation, ventral fins, a stronger wing spar, additional navigation and electronic equipment including ECM antenna bulges (of several different designs) on the vertical fin. The RF-8G was first flown by Vought Test Pilot, Joe Engle, on 31 August 1965. At this writing, one Reserve squadron still operates the RF-8G, VFP-206 based at NAF Washington, DC. Twenty-eight years of service life is respectable by any standards. Vought and the Navy have just reasons to be proud of their Crusader's record.

RF-8G (146873) of VFP-63 had nose gear failure while recovering aboard BON HOMME RICHARD (CVA-31). The Crusader was stopped by the barrier and the pilot escaped unharmed. C.1974 (US Navy via Pete Bowers)

(Below) RF-8G (145625) of VFP-206 turning up its engines on the Reserve Ramp at NAF Washington, DC. Trim colors are Maroon and White, the squadron insignia is located low on the fuselage directly under the cockpit. 24 April 1973 (Jim Sullivan)

RF-8G (146901) of VFP-63 was the last photo-Crusader to come off the assembly line. It was remanufactured in 1967 to RF-8G standards and assigned to NAS Miramar, CA. 21 October 1967 (Clay Jansson)

RF-8G (146858) of VFP-63 attached to HANCOCK (CVA-19) makes a full afterburner takeoff from NAF Atsugi, Japan. 1974 (Hideki Nagakubo)

RF-8G (145645) of VFP-63, Detachment Three, off MIDWAY (CVA-41). Low Visibility schemes were being adopted by the Navy in the mid-1970s. The modex 'NF' was on the tail (along with Granny). The Ram Air Turbine (RAT) is deployed from a compartment located under the National insignia. The forward camera bay is not in use. NAF Atsugi, Japan. April 1974 (Hideki Nagakubo)

(Below) RF-8G (146835) of VFP-63, Detachment Five, is assigned to CORAL SEA (CVA-43). Trim color is Dark blue and White. NAS Miramar, CA area. 1974 (Bob Lawson)

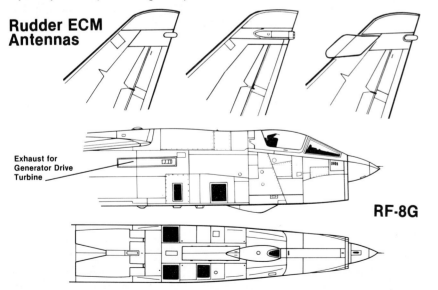

Rudder ECM Antennas

Exhaust for Generator Drive Turbine

RF-8G

(Right) RF-8G (146898) of VFP-306 flying a mission during the Photo Derby held at NAF Washington in April of 1981. (Don Spering/A.I.R.)

F-8H

In July of 1967, Vought started work on modernizing and remanufacturing the F-8D (F8U-2N) to the **F-8H** configuration and over the next twenty months a total of eighty-nine F-8D Crusaders were updated to H standards. The F-8H had underwing pylons added for carrying ordnance. An easily identifiable external feature was a 'hump' on the top of the fuselage over and forward of the wing, which housed a fire control system for the AGM-12 Bullpup missile. Also new was the addition of armor-plating and installation of a new wing which was engineered to deliver 4,000 hours of service life. The landing gear was strengthened, a longer nose gear was installed along with slightly smaller tires in all three positions. The F-8H incorporated additional electronic changes to improve its offensive capabilities. Vought insured better combat survivability with the separation of hydraulic power control lines. The first F-8H Crusader flight was on 17 July 1967 with John Konrad in the cockpit. During the air war in Vietnam, two F-8H Crusaders (147916 and 148710) from VF-51 were credited with kills of one MiG-21 each.

Its Sidewinder unfired, an F-8H (147043) of VF-51 returns to BON HOMME RICHARD (CVA-31) after a strike over Vietnam. The trim color on the rudder, fin and ventral fins was Red. 1968 (via Pete Bowers)

(Below) At the moment of touchdown, this F-8H of VF-211 smokes the deck of HANCOCK (CVA-19) in the South China Sea. 2 October 1968 (US Navy via Bill Curry)

(Above) F-8H (148691) of VF-51 is assigned to BON HOMME RICHARD (CVA-31). A Black area has been painted around the afterburner from the front of the cooling intakes aft. The Black area just over the missile rack and around the 20mm cannon ports was to minimize smoke stains. The fuselage 'hump' located over the wing area housed the fire control system for Bullpup missile. 20 January 1968 (Clay Jansson)

(Below) F-8H (148661) of VF-111 on the ramp after a passing rain shower. Colorful Red and White markings were applied to the nose, tail and wingtips. This aircraft was assigned to TICONDEROGA (CVA-14). 28 January 1969, NAS North Island. (Harry Gann via Clay Jansson)

'THUNDER', a F-8H (147916) of VFP-63 is assigned to training duties for West Coast pilots transitioning to the Crusader. This Crusader is a MiG killer, having bagged a MiG-21 while in the hands of VF-51 pilot, Lt Norman K McCoy on 1 August 1968. NAS Miramar, CA. 25 October 1969 (Clay Jansson)

F-8H (148643) of VF-162 from SHANGRI LA (CVA-38) on the flightline at NAS Miramar, CA. Yellow and Black markings trim this Crusader on the nose, wingtips and tail. 'Snoopy' riding a Sidewinder decorates the top of the fin. 14 March 1970 (Clay Jansson)

(Below) F-8H (148630) of VF-162 has just lifted off the runway at NAF Atsugi, Japan. This Crusader carries the older single missile launch rack. Trim markings are in Yellow and Black. The Bullpup control 'hump' on the spine of the F-8H can be seen outlined against the sky. 1970 (Hideki Nagakubo)

F-8H (147904) of VX-4 is from the Operational Test and Evaluation Squadron at NAS North Island, CA. The 'hump' on the spine of the fuselage over the wing houses the fire control system for the Bullpup missile and the installation forward of the windscreen is the AN/AAS-15 infra-red scanner for the Sidewinder missiles. McClellan AFB, CA. 23 October 1971 (Peter Mancus)

(Below) F-8H (147905) of VF-201 is on the flightline at NAS Dallas, TX. A fairing over an ECM antenna is located on the rear of the tail at the top of the rudder. This Texas Reserve Crusader is trimmed in Red outlined in Black. 6 April 1974 (Dr Carlton Eddy)

F-8P (F-8H) Philippine Crusader

Vought received a contract for twenty-five overhauled F8Hs in 1977. Withdrawn from storage at Davis-Montham Air Force Base, Arizona, twenty-five Crusaders were delivered to the Philippine Air Force under the designation F-8P. In addition, ten other aircraft were delivered to the Philippines to supply spare parts for ten years.

The TF-8A 'TWOSADER' was called back from NASA and used to help the Philippine pilots transition to the supersonic fighter. Unfortunately the TF-8A (143710) crashed at NAS Dallas on 28 July 1978 before finishing the program.

F-8P (F-8H) (148864) was one of twenty-five F-8Hs to be reconditioned and redesignated F-8P, and delivered to the Philippine Air Force in 1978. Basa AFB, PI 28 November 1979 (Sqn Leader Peter Russell-Smith)

F-8J

In January of 1968, Vought began the remanufacture of 136 F-8E (F8U-2NE) airframes into the highly modified **F-8J** version. The first of these flew on 31 January 1968. Perhaps the most unique modification to the Crusader was the introduction of Boundary Layer Control, a system which efficiently reduced the approach speed for carrier landings and the installation of the double-droop full-span leading edge. These innovations reduced the landing (and catapult) speed by fifteen knots as compared to the F-8E. The two underwing pylons provided extra fuel and/or ordnance capability when installed on the new 4,000 hour service-life wing. Like the F-8H, the F-8J had the beefed up landing gear with a longer nose gear, and slightly smaller tires. A larger horizontal stabilizer (flying tail) was installed and ECM bulges began to appear near the top of the vertical fin. The F-8J had a maximum speed of 950 knots with a service ceiling of 38,400 feet. and a combat radius of 382 nautical miles. Armament capability of the F-8J was unchanged from that of the F-8E. Vought completed remanufacturing of this version in late 1969.

(Above) F-8J (150661) of VF-124 was a MiG-Killer. On 19 May 1967, Lt (jg) Joseph Shea of VF-211, bagged a MiG-17. This Crusader has had underwing pylons installed. NAS Miramar, CA. 19 March 1970 (Clay Jansson)

(Left) F-8Js of VF-211 and F-8Hs of VF-24 head for the South China Sea and a WestPac combat cruise off Vietnam. Passing under the Golden Gate Bridge, HANCOCK (CVA-19) bids farewell to San Francisco. VF-211 is trimmed in Red and White, while VF-24 is Yellow and Black. 2 August 1969 (Bill Larkins)

(Below) F-8Js (150663 and 150918) of VF-191 break to port and head down to the deck for a landing aboard ORISKANY (CVA-34), during work-up prior to their WestPac cruise in Mid-1971. Trim color is Red. (US Navy via Bill Curry)

(Above) This F-8J (149164) is assigned to the Flight Test section of NATC Patuxent River, MD. The underwing pylons could haul ordnance or up to 600 gallons of additional fuel in two 300 gallon drop tanks. The insignia beneath the wing belongs to the Flight Test section. Trim color is red. NATC Patuxent River, MD. 23 April 1973 (Jim Sullivan)

(Below) This F-8J (150855) of VFP-63 was one of only a handful of Fighters assigned to a Photo-Recon squadron. After VF-124 was decommissioned, the remaining F-8 Station squadron was given the responsibility of training replacement F-8 pilots. Trim color is Red. NAS Miramar, CA. 12 May 1973 (Bob Lawson)

F-8K

In December of 1968, Vought started work on modernizing/remanufacturing eighty-seven F-8C models under the **F-8K** designation. Wing pylons (one under each wing) for carrying ordnance* and a new F-8E style cockpit interior and external lights. Part of the Navy's logic was to remanufacture and update its Crusaders so smaller aircraft carriers not capable of handling the larger F-4 Phantom II could be kept in service.

Recent information suggests that some of the F-8Cs flown in combat in Vietnam were field modified to take underwing pylons before the F-8K program made them standard.

(Above) F-8K (146952) of VMF-321 is parked on the Marine Reserve ramp at NAF Washington. Portable operations shack can be seen at the far right. Crusader 4 is being serviced prior to departure. 24 April 1973 (Jim Sullivan)

(Below) This F-8K (146947) was assigned to the US Naval Test Pilot School at NATC Patuxent River, MD. Trim color is Orange and Red. The last three digits of the BuNo serve as the aircraft number and are repeated on the nose. 21 April 1971 (Roger Besecker)

(Above) F-8K (F-8C) (147022) of VC-5 is configured for a landing at NAF Atsugi, Japan. Colorful Yellow and Red checkerboard is carried on the vertical stabilizer and rudder. 1969 (Hideki Nagakubo)

(Below) A rather heavily weathered F-8K (F-8C) (146941) of VMF-511 just before touching down on the runway at MCAS Cherry Point, NC. Trim color is Red with White stars. 13 April 1971 (Jim Sullivan)

(Above) This F-8K (146981), now of VMF-351, is a MiG-Killer. On 19 May 1967, while serving with VF-24, LCDR Bobby C Lee cut a MiG-17 in half with a Sidewinder. At the time of the kill this Crusader was a F-8C. NAF Washington, 24 April 1973 (Jim Sullivan)

F-8K Crusaders of VMF-351 formate with F-4B Phantom IIs of VMF-323, two sections and two generations of Marine fighters. By this time the Phantom II had almost completely taken over front line duty from the Crusader. 1974 (US Navy via Robert Carlisle)

F-8L(F-8B)

In December of 1968 Vought began modification of the F-8B (F8U-1E) Crusader with instrument changes and cockpit modifications that brought about an increase in night flying capabilities. New catapult keels were installed where necessary and approach power compensators were installed to assist in carrier landings. While ventral fins were not installed, provisions were made for them with attachment points. Sixty-one F-8Bs were rebuilt as F-8Ls.

(Above) Navy F-8L (145419), the remanufactured version of the F-8B, was assigned to Naval Air Test Facility Lakehurst, NJ. Installation of four 20MM cannon armament remained identical to the original production F8U-1's. The triangle on the tail was Yellow outlined in Black. 1972 (Bob Esposito)

(Left) F-8L (145451) Crusader carries the joint Reserve service designator NAVY/MARINE. The weathered condition of this Crusader attests to its heavy use. The guns are heavily smoked from firing. 7W was the station code for NAS Willow Grove Reserves. 8 April 1970 (Roger Besecker)

(Below) F-8L (145492) of VMF-321 was assigned to NAF Washington, DC and carries the Reserve modex 6A. Trim color on the weathered tail is Dark Blue. The fiberglass fairings under the squadron designation were attachment points provided (but never used) for the installation of ventral fins. August 1970 (Duane Kasulka via Clay Jansson)

F8U-3 Crusader III

As early as 1955, at the beginning of the F8U-1 program, Vought decided to begin work on what they felt would be Navy requirements for the next generation of fighters. The design team at Vought developed what they felt was a state-of-the-art interceptor. Similar in appearance to the F8U Crusader and designated the F8U-3 Crusader III, the machine was in fact a totally new aircraft, although many of the same features found in the F8U were incorporated. Bigger, with five feet more wingspan, over four feet more fuselage, and weighing nearly two tons more, the F8U-3 was considerably bigger than its predecessor. The Crusader III was powered by a Pratt and Whitney J75-P-4 engine that delivered 26,000 pounds of thrust with afterburner and with the addition of a 6,000 pound thrust Rocketdyne motor installed in the rear of the fuselage. But while the F8U-3 was test flown on a number of occasions (190 total flights for the three Crusader III prototypes), the rocket engine installation was never used. Projections called for a speed of MACH 3 to be obtained.

The variable incidence wing of the F8U Crusader was retained and Boundary Layer Control was incorporated. The cannon armament was deleted in favor of an all missile armament, with provisions being made for three Sparrow IIIs or three Sidewinders. The Crusader III had the capability of carrying ECM or photo-recon gear. The forward-raked chin airscoop was a multi-position design that varied the incoming shock wave angle to the engine for efficient operation. The Crusader III had automatic flight controls for holding a MACH number with the push of a button, was capable of operations in excess of 60,000 feet, and had a combat radius of close to 1,000 miles. Gross weight of the Crusader III, including 13,844 pounds of fuel, was 38,772 pounds.

A moveable pair of fuselage mounted ventral fins were fitted just forward of the flying tail. These fins were tied into the landing gear retraction system and were in a horizontal position when the landing gear was extended and when the landing gear was retracted, the fins descended into a near vertical position providing excellent stability at high speeds.

The first flight of the F8U-3 Crusader III was on 2 June 1958, when John Konrad flew a 48 minute flight at Edwards Air Force Base. The flight testing program developed few problems and much praise for the advanced aircraft. While possible windscreen failure prevented the Crusader III from reaching its maximum speed, it did reach Mach 2.6 (1760 mph) at 35,000 feet, and Vought engineers estimated that it would reach Mach 2.9.

The Chance Vought F8U-3 Crusader III was the final competition to the McDonnell Douglas F4H-1 Phantom II and compared favorably during testing at both NATC Patuxent River, MD and Edwards AFB, CA. While the Crusader III's performance was impressive, the two-engined, two-man crewed Phantom II was selected as the Navy's next generation first-line fighter in December of 1958.

Contracts called for eighteen Crusader III airframes to be built, however, only five were actually built and of those, only three were flown before the contracts were cancelled after the Phantom II was selected. Those built were 146340, 146341, 147085, 147086 and 147087. Shortly after the contract cancellation, all existing F8U-3 Crusader IIIs were turned over to NASA for high-altitude/high-speed research.

(Right) The F8U-3 Crusader III was a big aircraft attested to by the three men standing under the wing. Both the Sparrow III missiles and the nosewheel were offset to allow missile firing clearance. 1959 (Chance Vought via Art Schoeni)

(Above) Compare the size of the F8U-3 (141341) and F8U-1E (145438) on the Chance Vought ramp at Dallas, TX 1958 (Chance Vought via Art Schoeni)

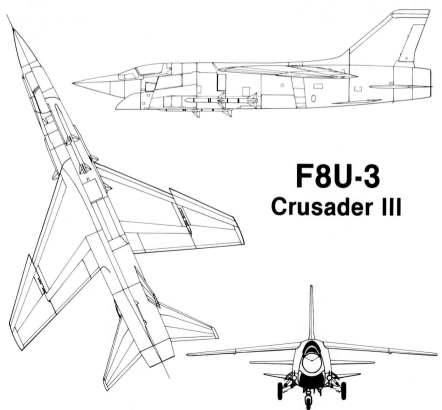

(Above) F8U-3 (146341) Crusader III was one of five Super-Crusaders built and flown in competition with the F4H-1 Phantom II. Even though it was capable of flying at speeds close to MACH 3, the Navy purchased the McDonnell product. NASA Facility, Langley AFB, VA. 26 September 1959 (Squadron Leader Peter Russell-Smith)

F8U-3
Crusader III

F8U-3 (147085) retracts its landing gear just after take off from NAS Dallas, TX. Orange trim was applied to the tail and outer wing panels. 1959 (Chance Vought via Art Schoeni)

NAVY AIR COLORS

SS6156 Navy Air Colors, Vol. 1

SS6157 Navy Air Colors, Vol. 2

Documenting the color schemes and markings of the U.S. Navy from the procurement of its first aircraft in 1911 through the end of WW II in 1945, NAVY AIR COLORS, Vol. 1 strikes new ground for historians, collectors, and model builders alike. Utilizing basic sources of data such as specifications, technical orders, letters, and memoranda, the authors have blended these facts with graphic and vivid photographs--photographs that are unique, clean, and accurately captioned.

The evolution of the color schemes and markings carried by aircraft and airships of the United States Navy, Marine Corps, and Coast Guard is further enhanced throughout the book by the splendidly detailed color artwork of Don Greer.

Among the craft and ships featured are Curtiss F6C-3, PD-1, and BFC-2, Vought SBU-1, Boeing F4B-1, Northrop BT-1, Grumman Bearcat and Tigercat.

Within the 97 pages, over 100 different aircraft are displayed, including 323 B&W photos, 6 color photos, 24 charts, and 154 full color paintings. (Soft Cover) $8.95

This is the second volume in the best-selling work on Navy Aircraft Colors that has filled a long standing gap in the annals of aviation history and presents the subject as only the authors and staff of Squadron/Signal could do it. After years of painstaking and exhaustive research based on both a myriad of Naval, Marine Corps, and Coast Guard regulations, and photographic evidence the authors have traced the development of the color changes, color scheme changes and marking changes. Much new material has been unearthed and is presented here for the first time. The colors, schemes and markings are fully documented in both text, photographs, and personal experience. Only in this and in VOLUME ONE can one find the material in one easy to use place.

From the Glossy Sea Blue of Hellcats, Corsairs, Bearcats, PB4Ys and Mariners in the immediate post World War II and Korean War; the Cutlasses, Demons and Banshees, that began the Light Gull Gray over Glossy Insignia White through the Corsair IIs and Phantoms that are ending it; up to and including the Corsair IIs, Skyhawks, and the new Marine Corps Hornet in its tactical scheme with *low viz* markings of today. truly a necessity for a complete aviation library.

Volume Two contains 96 pages with 18 pages of color including covers, 63 full color paintings, 59 full color photographs, and 217 Black and White photographs. . . . . (Soft Cover) $8.95

squadron/signal publications